MW01615969

Speaking God's Language

Joni Eareckson Tada

ROSE PUBLISHING/ASPIRE PRESS

Torrance, California

Prayer: Speaking God's Language
© Copyright 2014 Joni Eareckson Tada

Aspire Press, an imprint
of Rose Publishing, Inc.
4733 Torrance Blvd., #259
Torrance, California 90503 USA
www.rose-publishing.com
www.aspirepress.com

All Scripture quotations, unless otherwise indicated, are taken from the Holy Bible, New International Version®. NIV®. Copyright © 1973, 1978, 1984 by International Bible Society. Used by permission of Zondervan. All rights reserved.

Printed by Regent Publishing Services Ltd.
Printed in China
May 2014, 2nd printing

Contents

The Author

Joni Eareckson Tada, the founder and chief executive officer of Joni and Friends International Disability Center, is an international advocate for people with disabilities. A diving accident in 1967 left Joni Eareckson, then 17,  a quadriplegic in a wheelchair. After two years of rehabilitation, she emerged with new skills and a fresh determination to help others in similar situations. She founded Joni and Friends in 1979 to provide Christ-centered programs to special needs families, as well as training to churches. Through the organization's *Christian Institute on Disability*, Joni and her team have helped develop disability ministry courses of study in major Christian universities and seminaries. Visit us at www.joniandfriends.org.

Using the Word of God in Your Prayers

The large window in the airport framed a gray afternoon. Our flight was late and my friends Judy and Bunny stood beside me to pray—something we often do before and after flights. I was feeling discouraged by the news that we lacked the funds to launch an outreach to help disabled children in several eastern European orphanages.

Bunny reached for our hands, we closed our eyes, and she prayed, "Lord, send forth the corn and the wine and the oil. Send forth the early rains… the late rains… and produce a wonderful crop of blessings…" I recognized words from Joel 2:19 in her prayer: "The LORD will reply to them: 'I am sending you grain, new wine and oil, enough to satisfy you fully…'" I wondered if Bunny was thinking about the needed ministry funds.

Just then, I felt someone edge between us. The mystery person must have been a believer; he kept punctuating Bunny's prayer with "Amens." When we finished, he picked up his bag to run and catch his flight. Before he left, he folded a $100 bill into Bunny's hand. As he hurried away, Bunny waved the bill in the air like a flag of victory and said, "Yea, even while I was speaking in prayer, the angel came with the answer!"

She was right. When Bunny prays, things happen. "Joni," she instructed as she tucked the bill in my coat pocket, "This is the first fruits of what God will supply!" And it was. A foundation eventually caught our vision and helped fund the outreach to the orphanages. I've learned, through years of interceding with her, that Bunny's prayers not only seem to, but do, have power with God. It's because she has learned to pray in the language of the Father.

Even her response was from Daniel 9:21, "Yea, even while I was speaking in prayer."

Why Use God's Word in Our Prayers?

As Christians, we all wish to exhibit greater faith in prayer. How do we gain greater faith? Romans 10:17 provides the answer, "Faith comes from hearing the message, and the message is heard through the word of Christ."

I have learned to follow Bunny's lead and salt-and-pepper my prayers with the Word of God. It's a way of employing God's language when we talk to him. The Bible underscores two things that God honors above all else: his name and his Word. "I will exalt you, my God the King; I will praise your name for ever and ever... for you have exalted above all things your name and your word" (Ps. 145:1; Ps. 138:2). When we bring God's Word directly into our praying, we are bringing God's power into our praying.

♥ "The word of God is living and active. Sharper than any double-edged sword…" (Heb. 4:12). God's Word gives our prayers life, infusing vitality into our praises and petitions, as well as the thoughts that frame our petitions.

♥ "'Is not my word like fire,' declares the Lord, 'and like a hammer that breaks a rock in pieces?'" (Jer. 23:29). To use God's Word in prayer is to employ divine power in breaking strongholds and demolishing arguments of the enemy.

♥ "And we also thank God continually because, when you received the word of God, which you heard from us, you accepted it not as the word of men, but as it actually is, the word of God, which is at work in you who believe" (1 Thess. 2:13). If God's Word works in our lives, think how much more it works in our prayers.

Scripture Makes Us Think When We Pray

♥ It shows God we have thought through our praises and petitions and aligned them with the plumb line of Scripture.

♥ It shows him the importance we are attaching to our requests. It demonstrates the high regard and appreciation we attach to his Word.

♥ It underscores that we desire to search out his heart in a matter and seek to know his will.

"There are only three classes of people in the world today: those who are afraid, those who do not know enough to be afraid, and those who know their Bibles."

—Unknown preacher

Plumb line:

Cord with a weight on one end used to determine a straight, vertical line.

Stories of Saints
Who Used Scriptures in Their Prayers

Habakkuk

This remarkable prophet appealed to God on the basis of his Word during a time of deep national distress—the ruthless Babylonian army was poised to sweep across the country like water from a ruptured dam. Yes, the prophet agreed with the Lord that Judah was deserving of his judgment. But how could God use a people even more evil than they as his rod of discipline? Habakkuk echoed the sentiments of Scriptures of old when he wrote, "Your eyes are too pure to look on evil; you cannot tolerate wrong. Why then do you tolerate the treacherous? Why are you silent while the wicked swallow up those more righteous than themselves?" (Hab. 1:13).

David

This king was the most beloved ruler of Israel, "a man after his [God's] own heart," as 1 Samuel 13:14 describes him. When David prayed, he pleaded God's character on the basis of what he knew to be true about the Lord from his Word: "Remember, O Lord, your great mercy and love, for they are from of old…according to your love remember me, for you are good, O Lord" (Ps. 25:6–7). Does it sound cheeky or presumptuous to remind God of his Word? Nevertheless, the Lord wants us to claim his love, plead his holiness, remind him of his goodness, recount his longsuffering, present to him his steadfastness, and pray in his power. After all, Isaiah 1:18 assures, "'Come now, let us reason together,' says the Lord."

Solomon

It was Solomon's privilege to build a great temple to God in Jerusalem. When it came time to dedicate the temple, the wisest man who ever lived humbled himself and knelt down before the whole assembly of Israel. "He said: 'O LORD, God of Israel, there is no God like you in heaven or on earth—you who keep your covenant of love with your servants who continue wholeheartedly in your way…. Now LORD, God of Israel, keep for your servant David my father the promises you made to him when you said, "You shall never fail to have a man to sit before me on the throne of Israel, if only your sons are careful in all they do to walk before me according to my law, as you have done." And now, O LORD, God of Israel, let your word that you promised your servant David come true'" (2 Chron. 6:14–17). Solomon appealed to God to be faithful to the promises he had made King David.

Reflect

Search the words of God's prophets and kings—look for instances in the Bible where people prayed using other passages from Scripture.

Deeper Prayer

Often I attend prayer meetings where various requests are made for healing, finances, safety in travel, or job promotions. It's natural that people would want prayer for good health, financial blessing, a safe flight, and a better job—and it's natural for friends to pray that way. But a closer look at God's Word reveals deeper and more divinely inspired ways to pray about health and finances and jobs.

♥ Is there a life-threatening illness? Prayer for healing is definitely in order, but so are the robust blessings of Psalm 119:140, "Your promises have been thoroughly tested, and your servant loves them." How much richer it is to pray, "Lord, this cancer is testing your promises in the life of my friend who is ill, but you are faithful to every promise you've made to her. May my friend come to truly love your promises through this time of testing."

♥ **Is there a need for finances?** Prayer for needed funds is in order, but so are the rewards of Proverbs 15:17, "Better a meal of vegetables where there is love than a fattened calf with hatred." You could choose to pray, "Lord, financial blessing isn't the focus; your Word says that love should be. May we learn to 'live on little' if it means leaning harder on you, as well as each other."

♥ **Is there a need for understanding?** Prayer for emotional support from friends and family is reasonable, but let's remember that our Savior was misunderstood by his closest friends. Luke 17:25 says, "But first he must suffer many things and be rejected by this generation." Perhaps it's wiser to pray, "Lord, although I long for understanding from friends, help me to have your attitude of love toward those who misunderstood and rejected you."

♥ Is there a wish for a bigger, newer home? We all want to move up in the world, but remember Jesus' example in Luke 9:58, "Foxes have holes and birds of the air have nests, but the Son of Man has no place to lay his head." Try praying, "Lord, no servant should be above his Master, so convict me if I'm merely 'keeping up with the Jones's.' Help me to minimize my desires, gladly examine our needs in the light of our budget, and show us how to live in a way that reflects your priorities."

♥ Is there a desire to serve in missions overseas? Although it's true that Jesus said in Matthew 28:19 to "go and make disciples of all nations," he may want you to first "love your neighbor" closer to home (Matt. 19:19). You could choose to pray, "Father, there are people of every culture and language residing in my own city who are utterly lost. Before I ask you to send me far away, help me be a missionary in my own town."

♥ Are there hopes to seek an advanced degree in school? Asking God to guide a student is appropriate, but what about seeking God's timing? Ecclesiastes 12:11–12 says, "The words of the wise are … like firmly embedded nails—given by one Shepherd. Be warned, my son, of anything in addition to them. Of making many books there is no end, and much study wearies the body." It's always wise to pray, "Lord, as I consider graduate school, help me put into practice all the wisdom gleaned from your Word and from the wise advisors you have placed around me. Help me discern your calling for my life."

♥ Is there a need for reconciliation in a marriage? Asking God that a spouse see the error of his or her ways might be appropriate, but God may want to start with the one asking. First Corinthians 13 from *The Message* says: "Love… doesn't keep score of the sins of others, doesn't revel when others grovel, takes pleasure in the flowering of truth, puts up with anything, trusts God always, always looks for the best, never looks back, but keeps going to the end" (vv. 5–7). How much more insightful to pray, "Father, help my friend not to keep a record of her husband's wrongs; may she look for the best in him;

may she first examine her own heart to see if there is any offensive attitude on her part."

It's the way I pray for children who have disabilities. I keep in mind Matthew 19:14–15: "Jesus said, 'Let the little children come to me, and do not hinder them, for the kingdom of heaven belongs to such as these.' When he had placed his hands on them, he went on from there." A verse like that inspires me to pray: "Lord Jesus, your heart went out to children when you walked on earth. I can picture you tousling their hair, bouncing them on your knee, and laying your hands on their heads to give a blessing. If your heart went out to the boys and girls who could walk up to you, how much more must your heart overflow toward little Jeanette with spina bifida or Benjamin who has cerebral palsy? Today, may they feel your hand of blessing on them."

Language Lessons

Bunny is a good instructor on how to pray using Scripture. Her good friend, Dick Eastman, has also spent a lifetime cultivating the discipline of employing the language of the Bible in his prayers. Dick has wonderful suggestions in his book, *The Hour that Changes the World*. Here's a good way to get started:

♥ Read portions of God's Word, not necessarily as Bible study, but to search for insights which might be applied to petitions or praises.

♥ Meditate on portions that reveal a particular truth to be used during prayer time. Evaluate how the passage might translate into a specific petition, asking yourself, *Does this verse prompt me to pray for someone with such a need? Is it possible*

to use some of the words of this Scripture,
word for word, as I pray?

♥ Form a personal prayer enriched by
the passage. Here's an example. Suppose
your brother is feeling as though his life
is over since his wife died. One morning
you're reading Philippians 1:6, "He who
began a good work in you will carry it
on to completion until the day of Christ
Jesus." Meditate on the passage. It may
occur to you that this biblical truth is just
what your brother needs.

So you pray, "Lord, I grab hold of this
passage on behalf of my brother. Help
him to see the good work you want
to accomplish in his life through his
heartache. Carry your purposes in his life
to completion. I know you'll be faithful
to this promise you've given him in
Philippians 1:6, and although my brother

may be too depressed to pray this way for himself, I hold you to your Word as I bring his needs before you."

Reflect

Read Colossians 1:9–12 and insert the name of a loved one in place of the pronouns in the passage. Prayers voiced from this passage not only bring about fundamental changes in the people and situations for which you pray, but such prayer keeps you on balance with God's priorities.

If you need fresh words for confession of your sin, read Psalm 51. Picture yourself on your knees before the throne of God. As you read each verse, let the Holy Spirit reveal areas of your life that need confession.

The Best Prayer Book You Own

The Bible is our prayer book and we'd be amiss to neglect its riches. The Bible is full of language lessons so we might enjoy Word-enriched prayer. It's the key to finding God's will when we pray, providing balance and meaning. Great themes abound—God's holiness, wisdom, faithfulness, sovereignty, love, and mercy—all of which beautify our praises, adorn our intercessions, embroider our petitions, and give weight and significance to every supplication.

Most of all, using the Word of God in prayer is about as close as we can get to the Living Word, the Lord Jesus. If we're going to pray in his name, it makes sense to speak in his language.

Charles Spurgeon was a noted leader who literally "prayed" the Word of God. He expressed,

"Every promise of scripture is a writing of God which may be pleaded before him with this reasonable request, 'Do as thou hast said!' The Creator will not cheat the creature who depends upon his truth; and far more, the Heavenly Father will not break his word to his own child."

Praying Scripture Changes Things—and You

The more you center in prayer on God's Word, the more its power and life becomes not only a part of those for whom you pray; it also becomes part of you.

- ♥ Focus on quoting God's mercies in prayer as David did, and you will become more merciful.

- ♥ Concentrate on the Cross when you pray, and you'll become more forgiving.

- ♥ Hearken to the confessions of Jeremiah and Isaiah in prayer and your conscience will become more sensitive to evil.

- ♥ Quote Paul's example in your prayers, and you won't try to rationalize or explain away your sin.

♥ Plead with God about his wisdom, quoting Proverbs 4, and you will become wiser. Continue to plead, and you'll also gain knowledge, understanding, discernment, and prudence.

♥ Lace your worship with psalms of praise and you will experience the joy of worship.

♥ Center your requests around his holiness and you will grow in holiness.

E. M. Bounds was a saint of God known for his extraordinary prayer life. A lawyer during the Civil War, Bounds spent an average of four hours in prayer every morning. Immediately following prayer, he would write his most intimate prayer experiences. Like other spiritual leaders of his generation, Bounds discovered the tremendous value of applying God's Word in his prayers.

He once testified,

"The Word of God is the fulcrum upon which the lever of prayer is placed, and by which things are mightily moved. God has committed Himself, his purpose, and his promise to prayer. His Word becomes the basis, the inspiration of our praying, and there are circumstances under which by importunate prayer, we may obtain an enlargement of his promises."

—E. M. Bounds, The Possibilities of Prayer

Importunate:
extremely persistent, never giving up.

An Enlargement of
His Promises

E. M. Bounds was right. When we use Scripture in prayer, we not only receive an enlargement of his promises but a greater degree of faith in our prayers, as well as a more glorious perspective on God's grand scheme of things.

I once received an "enlargement of his promises" from Scripture praying. It was in the early 1980s, shortly after my honeymoon with my new husband, Ken. A couple of months into our marriage I realized that Ken preferred to spend Monday nights in front of the TV with chips, salsa, and the NFL rather than be "my hands" to write out my Bible study. *Horrors,* I thought, *he's not a "man of the Word"!* Back then, we didn't realize our situation was typical for newlyweds; we suffered through the normal unmet expectations, bruised feelings, and verbal spats.

I was itching to change my husband, but all my nagging only made things worse. Feeling discouraged, I perused God's Word for help and stumbled across Philippians 2:3–4, "Do nothing out of selfish ambition or vain conceit, but in humility consider others better than yourselves. Each of you should look not only to your own interests, but also to the interests of others." I realized, *I want Ken to change for selfish reasons... so that he'll meet my expectations. To be honest, I don't consider him "better than myself"; I feel like I'm the one who's in the right—like I've got it spiritually together, not him.*

A Greater Faith

The closer I looked at Philippians 2:3–4, the more I felt convicted. It catapulted me into a major prayer advance for Ken. I sincerely wanted to follow God's Word and have humility of mind, as well as to regard my husband as better than myself. How could I look out for his interests? I flipped through the Bible until I found a passage that seemed suitable as a basis for prayer for my husband.

I meditated on Psalm 24:3–10 and looked for ideas and words I could employ in prayer for my husband. I would spend evenings in our bedroom, praying, "Jesus, you want Ken to stand in your holy place, to have clean hands and a pure heart. May you cause him to lift up his soul to you and receive your blessing. May he seek your face. The gates of Ken's heart are a little rusty and the hinges aren't used to opening up to you…. Lift up the gates of Ken's heart that you, the King of Glory, might come in! Lord, say to him, "I, the King of Glory, will come in and rule your life—I, the Lord, strong and mighty. I pray this for my husband whom I love."

A Glorious Perspective

I can't tell you how many times I interceded for Ken using Psalm 24 and other passages. Now, many years later, it's clear that Christ sits on the throne of my husband's heart. Ken also has memorized many more verses of Scripture than I have! One summer he committed to memory the entire Sermon on the Mount— that's several chapters in the Gospel of Matthew! When we're together driving in the van, often Ken will recite Matthew, chapters 5–7 (it takes him nearly 20 minutes). I have listened to him say the Sermon on the Mount so many times that I nearly have the first chapter committed to heart as well! Perhaps at one time I thought Ken wasn't a man of God's Word—but not now.

Something else is clear: Ken still loves football. What has changed is that I enjoy it with him! Years ago when I prayed Psalm 24 over my husband, believing that God would change him, God did much more. He changed me. It was, as E. M. Bounds would say, "an enlargement of his promises."

I'm convinced Ken and I are still feeling the repercussions of all that Scripture praying; it's because it was based on Psalm 24 and was alive, active, and powerful, bringing about fundamental changes in my heart where it counted most—and also in the heart of dear Ken.

Small Scriptures...
A Big Impact!

Sometimes the tiniest snippets of prayer from Scripture can be the most powerful.

Picture the scene: When Jesus entered the home of Simon Peter and learned his mother-in-law was sick, the people made a beautiful and simple request. Luke 4:38 records that request: "Jesus left the synagogue and went to the home of Simon. Now Simon's mother-in-law was suffering from a high fever, and they asked Jesus to help her." Did you catch it? Help her.

There was no fanfare, no digging deep into the matter, no extended discussions and wondering if it was the will of God or not. Jesus was under their roof and they knew he had the power to help a sick woman.

Help Her!

Sometimes it's hard to know what or how to pray. Ken and I have felt that way lately. For several months, we have been praying nightly for a list of friends who have cancer. Some of the cases are pretty extensive; others look hopeful. Through it all, our friends are struggling through pain and disappointment. Often we don't know how to pray, but we can't go wrong using the simple scriptural words of Luke 4:38, "Lord, help her." It's straightforward, to-the-point, direct and sincere. Jesus is under the roof in the homes of our friends and we don't have to dig deep into the matter or question God's will—after all, God knows best what would be helpful.

Save Me!

Another short Scripture prayer is found in Matthew 14:30. It's the story of when Peter got out of the boat and walked on the water toward Jesus. "But when he saw the wind, he was afraid and, beginning to sink, cried out, 'Lord, save me!'" Again, there is no fanfare or digging deep into the matter. Sometimes when you find yourself confused and bewildered, borrow those three short, sincere words from Peter. Muse on his desperation for the Savior. Feel his need of a Deliverer. Then cry out from the bottom of your heart, "Lord, save me!"

There's something else I like about those Scriptures. "Lord, help her!" and "Lord, save me!" sum up our bewilderment. They describe how we've come to the end of our understanding and that we have no one else to whom we can turn. To pray, "Lord, help her!" or "Lord, save me!" is to have your focus on Jesus.

Reflect

How can a prayer be short, but also carry power and importance?

Read Matthew 6:7. Think how this warning might shape your future prayers.

Praying in the Name of Jesus

Let's consider what it means to pray in the name of Jesus.

Shortly before he was led to the cross, our Savior said, "I will do whatever you ask in my name… you may ask me for anything in my name, and I will do it" (John 14:13–14). These are profound words from the lips of Jesus. What does that mean for us? Surely, it means more than saying "In Jesus' name" at the end of a prayer.

♥ To pray in the name of Jesus is to pray admitting that God hears me only because I'm the guest of his Son. It's to pray in the bold but respectful way that Jesus did while on earth.

♥ To pray in Jesus' name means we ask God for the things Jesus taught us to ask. He summarizes them in the Lord's Prayer: spiritual things, eternal things. "May your kingdom spread... May your plans be accomplished on this rebellious planet... Forgive the way I've treated you... Keep me from falling for the evil that allures me" (See Matt. 6:9–13). Only one request in six deals with earthbound matters, and even there he taught us to pray, "Give us this day our daily bread" —not, "Bless the Dow Jones Average and please be with the NASDAQ in the next financial quarter."

Of course it's not wrong to pray beyond our basic needs— to pray that Susie will find her lost kitten, that none of us will catch colds this winter, and that Christmas will hurry up and get here. God loves to hear preschool children pray. Jesus also invites grownups to "cast all your anxiety on him," and "present your requests to God" (1 Pet. 5:7; Phil. 4:6). But do we really think Jesus gave us a blank check for an easy life? Do we imagine we can pray our way clear of trials? Think again: "… in your thinking be adults" (1 Cor. 14:20).

♥ To pray in the name of Christ is to pray in a way that reflects his character and his priorities. It is to pray with his agenda in mind. The whole purpose behind Christ's coming was to spread the message that sin kills, hell is real, God is merciful, his kingdom can save us, and Christ is our passport. May all our prayers reflect these core values that Jesus held dearly when he offered his prayers to the Father.

"God of our life, there are days when the burdens we carry chafe our shoulders and weigh us down; when the road seems dreary and endless, the skies gray and threatening; when our lives have no music in them, and our hearts are lonely and our souls have lost courage. Flood the path with light, we beseech Thee; turn our eyes to where the skies are full of promise; tune our hearts to brave music; give us the sense of comradeship with heroes and saints of every age; and so quicken our spirits that we may be able to encourage the souls of all who journey with us on the road of life, to Thy honor and glory. In Jesus' name, Amen."

—St. Augustine (450 AD)

"Father, we thank Thee that dark and uncertain is our future; because in darkness and doubt we must cling more closely to Thee. Father, we thank Thee that there will be pain; because through pain we are forced to clutch at Thy hand. Father, we thank Thee that there will be loneliness; because in loneliness Thou art more surely our friend. Father, we thank Thee that there shall be death; because in dying we come unto Thee."

—John Hoyland (1830–1894)

Reflect

Many great hymns of the faith contain solid doctrinal truths. What hymns do you know that reflect truths from Scripture?

Consider memorizing several hymns so you might include the words in your prayers.

The team at Joni and Friends want to encourage you in your life of prayer. We invite you to join our Joni and Friends Prayer Team of several hundred prayer warriors who, like yourself, have a heart for prayer. Thousands of people with disabilities and their families need prayer; plus, many of our Joni and Friends' programs need to be bathed in intercession. We understand that if prayer does not cover an outreach, then nothing of any lasting, eternal good will be accomplished. So learn to speak God's language with us here at Joni and Friends—consider joining our Prayer Team by visiting www.joniandfriends.org.

Books by Joni Eareckson Tada

The topics of fear and hopelessness, depression and suffering, loneliness and worry are issues that author Joni Eareckson Tada can speak to personally. Let Joni tell you her secrets to peace and joy. She knows that God does not take pleasure in seeing you suffer. He has compassion for you and gives you many ways to deal with life's pain so that you can have peace.

Making Sense of Suffering

When you're overwhelmed by pain and problems, it's easy to feel helpless, hopeless, and sinking into a whirlpool of self-pity. Joni Eareckson Tada knows about these emotions first hand. Joni shares biblical insights that bring hope and comfort to those who are trying to make sense of their suffering.

Paperback, 4" x 6", 48 pages, ISBN 9781628620467

God's Hand in Our Hardship

When you read through the Bible, you can see that God hates suffering. So why doesn't our all-powerful God get rid of suffering? Joni Eareckson Tada tackles the big questions about suffering: How can a gracious and loving God allow anyone to suffer? Why do "good" people have to suffer? What possible good can come through suffering?

Paperback, 4"x 6", 48 pages, ISBN 9781628620474

Breaking the Bonds of Fear

Is fear causing you to lose sleep, stress out, and worry? When Joni Eareckson Tada experienced a tragic accident that left her quadriplegic, fear gripped her life. Joni explains the steps she took—and still takes daily—to grow in confidence in the Lord and break the bonds of fear.

Paperback, 4"x 6", 48 pages, ISBN 9781628620481

Prayer: Speaking God's Language

How can we draw closer to God in prayer? How can we "speak God's language"? As Christians grow in the discipline of praying, it becomes clear that there is always more to learn. Joni Eareckson Tada shares personal stories and insights that will help you hone your skill of praying with the Word of God.

Paperback, 4"x 6", 48 pages, ISBN 9781628620498

Available at www.aspirepress.com or wherever good Christian books are sold.